William Paine Sheffield

A Historical Sketch of Block Island

William Paine Sheffield

A Historical Sketch of Block Island

ISBN/EAN: 9783744733373

Printed in Europe, USA, Canada, Australia, Japan

Cover: Foto ©Thomas Meinert / pixelio.de

More available books at **www.hansebooks.com**

HISTORICAL SKETCH

—OF—

BLOCK ISLAND.

By WILLIAM P. SHEFFIELD.

A

HISTORICAL SKETCH

OF

BLOCK ISLAND,

BY

WILLIAM P. SHEFFIELD.

––––––––––

NEWPORT:

JOHN P. SANBORN & CO., MERCURY OFFICE, PRINTERS.

1876.

BLOCK ISLAND.

CHAPTER I.

This Island belonged to the Narragansetts, and its Indian name was Manisses.

A writer in the North American Review informs us that it was visited by Varrazano, in 1524, who thought it resembled the Isle of Rhodes. He called it Claudia, in honor of the mother of his patron, Francis I, Emperor of France.

In 1526 Gomez entered Narragansett Bay and of course must have seen, if he did not visit, this Island.

Adrian Block, in 1614, on the banks of the Hudson, built the first decked vessel built in the American Colonies; she was called " The Yacht. "

De Laet, in his voyages, says that "Adrian Block, a Dutch navigator, sailed Eastward through the Sound and discovered several Islands, the last of which he called after his own name."

Isaac de Rasier, who went from the Dutch settlement at Manhaddoes, to visit Plymouth, in 1626, entered Narragansett Bay, which he called "Sloups Bay," and, from some point above Fall River, embarked and crossed to Plymouth. He must have seen this Island, and in his report to his home government, he says that the Dutch were already carrying on a prosperous trade with the Indians on this bay, so that this Island was probably then well known to his countrymen. De Rasier says that the trading with these Indians by the Dutch was a source of uneasiness with the people of Plymouth at this time.

The English from Massachusetts visited the Island, for purposes of trade, as early as 1636; 5th month, 20th of that year, one John Oldham, who had been banished from Plymouth, and had taken up his residence in Watertown, was killed by the Indians at the Island, upon his return, accompanied by two English boys, from a trading expedition to the Pequot country.

Lion Gardner says that the Indians of the Island traded with the Dutch the gold pieces of which they robbed Oldham. John Gallop discovered Oldham's boat, on board of which were fifteen or sixteen Indians, eleven of whom he frightened so that they jumped overboard and were drowned, one was afterwards thrown overboard after he was bound for fear that he might get loose and do some mischief, and probably the others concluded to follow their companions.

The murder of Oldham was brought to the notice of Canonicus, who sent Miantinomah with two hundred Indians to take revenge on the Island Indians for the offence. Miantinomah recovered the two English boys and delivered them to Roger Williams who sent them home to Massachusetts. Miantinomah also arrested two of the Indians who were engaged in the murder, one of whom died suddenly and the other was delivered to the authorities in Massachusetts to be taught a lesson in the habits of civilized life, which, if the Indian ever comprehended, he soon forgot.

Massachusetts fitted out an expedition of ninety men under John Underhill, Nathaniel Turner and Captain Jennyson, over whom was John Endicott, and commissioned this expedition to put to death the Indians at the Island, and to bring away the women and children. When the expedition arrived at the Island, the Indians made some show of resistance, but soon fled to the woods, which contained no good timber. The English could not find the Indians but found two plantations, three miles asunder. and about sixty wigwams, some of which were very large and fair, and about two hundred acres of Indian corn, some of which was gathered and laid in heaps. The English remained two days at the Island, and burned the wigwams and mats and some of the corn, and stove the canoes of the Indians, and departed.

The Rev. Samuel Niles, in his History of the French and Indian Wars, says that long before the English settled the Island, and perhaps before there was any white settlement in this land, as he was told by some of the old men among the Indians, when the Mohegans and the Narragansetts were at war, the Indians started from the Island, one clear moonlight night, to go to the Mohegan country to attack their enemies; that they had not gone far from the Island when in the glade of the moon the Island Indians saw the canoes of the Mohegan Indians coming in the direction of the Island. The Island Indians immediately put back to the Island, and landed near a swamp on the South-west part of the Island and drew their canoes into the swamp where they

hid themselves and waited until the Mohegan warriors landed and marched past into the Island, then the Island Indians
destroyed the canoes of their enemies, and followed the
Mohegan warriors, and finally surrounded them on the top
of a high bluff on the South-east part of the Island, and there
held them until they were exhausted and died of starvation.

This Island was claimed to be a part of Massachusetts, no
doubt by conquest, up to the granting to Rhode Island of
the charter by Charles II, which was accepted in 1663.

October 19th, 1658, the General Court of Massachusetts
granted this Island to Governor John Endicott, in consideration of his great services to the country; to Richard
Bellingham, Deputy Governor, for his good services ; to Major
General Daniel Dennison, in respect to his great pains in
transcribing the laws, and to Major William Hawthorne, in
regard to his surrendering seven hundred acres of land
granted him; to each one quarter part.

From the narrative of the Commissioners from England
to New England we learn that John Alcock, a physician,
having bought Block Island of some of Boston, who took
upon them power never granted them to sell it, desireth that
he may not be dispossessed of it. The Royal Commissioners
lost Alcock's petition, but I am not aware that any effort
was ever made to dispossess Alcock and his associates of the
Island, if, indeed, the Island was not guaranteed to its
purchasers by the charter.

August 7th, 1660, Simon Ray, Thomas Terry, Thomas
Faxon, Hugh Williams, Samuel Dearing, Richard Ellis, Peter
George and Philip Wharton, met at the house of John
Alcock in Roxbury to confer about the purchase of Block
Island, and they agreed with Alcock to purchase the Island
proportionally They also had a consultation about erecting

a plantation thereon ; they considered the remoteness of the place, the cost by land and sea, and that it could not be settled without great charge. Then some began to decline, but the remainder proceeded and voted that all concerned in the land should be at equal charge in the expense of the settlement.

John Alcock, Philip Wharton, Hugh Williams, Thomas Terry, Samuel Dearing and Simon Ray undertook the building of a barque for the transportation of cattle to the Island. Simon Ray, Thomas Terry and Samuel Dearing should build the hull, and John Alcock, Hugh Williams and Philip Wharton should provide the sails and rigging. And considering there was no harbor Simon Ray and Samuel Dearing built a shallop, at their own cost, for the quicker and better transportation of passengers. William Rose was master of the barque, and William Edwards and Samuel Staples undertook the sailing of the shallop around the cape.

In the beginning of April, 1661, the barque sailed from Braintree, and the shallop received its passengers at Taunton. The passengers embraced the nine persons that met at Dr. Alcock's.

The next proprietors' meeting was held the following September, 1st Tuesday, at the house of Philip Wharton in Boston. They chose Mr. Noyes their surveyor to divide their lands, and took into consideration the subject of the maintenance of a minister, and voted that a proportion of their land should be laid out for that purpose and to continue for that use forever. The narration, of which this is the substance, extended in detail, remains upon the records of this ancient township in the handwriting of Simon Ray.

By a deed made by Thomas Terry to certain Indian chiefs, dated March 8th, 1663, it appears that John Alcock, Peter Tallman, Samuel Dearing and Thomas Terry had purchased the Indian title to the entire Island.

It may be worthy of remark here that the name of Rose, the commander of the barque, is the only name of a first settler which is represented among the present population of the Island. It is highly probable that some of the purchasers never removed their families to the Island. In 1662, James Sands, who had formerly resided in Portsmouth, which place he left with Ann Hutchinson for whom he attempted to build a house at East Chester in New York, but was driven away by the Indians, united in the settlement at Block Island. He built there a stone house to which the inhabitants were in the habit of resorting for protection in times of danger. Joseph Kent of Swansey joined the settlement either in 1662 or 1663.

Block Island was settled by Massachusetts Puritans, and with the exception perhaps of James Sands, had but little sympathy with the people or the institutions of Rhode Island, and upon the authority of the grandson of Mr. Sands, he did not differ in religious belief from the other settlers on the Island.

At the March session of the General Assembly, 1664, the governor and deputy governor were desired to declare unto their friends, the inhabitants of Block Island, that they were under the care of the General Assembly, and that they admit not any other to have rule over them, and that James Sands, who was a freeman of the colony, be requested to come to the governor and deputy governor to take his engagement as constable and conservator of the peace, and that the most able and deserving men be warned into the next court, in May, to be informed of their privileges and to be made free of the colony.

At the May session, James Sands and Joseph Kent petitioned the Assembly, in behalf of themselves and their associates, that the householders on the Island be admitted free of the colony. Roger Williams, Thomas Olney and James Torry were appointed by the Assembly to draw up their thoughts, and commit them to the Assembly for its further approbation with reference to the preserving his majesty's peace at the Island.

At the same session of the Assembly, Sands and Kent and Thomas Terry presented a petition ancilliary to the one first presented. To these petitions the General Assembly made the reply contained in the Colonial Records, Vol. II, p 53, etc. The Assembly accepted the list of freemen, commissioned Sands and Terry to call the inhabitants, mentioned in the petition, together, and to read to them the orders of the court for their present regulation, to inform them that they were to be owned as freemen. That Messrs. Sands and Kent were to take from the inhabitants a writing under their hands, that they appointed them (S. and K.) to request the court to admit them as freemen and that they then desired the same. That they would bear due faith and allegiance to his majesty, Charles II, his heirs and successors. That they would yield obedience to the colony, and a record was to be made of the names of the freemen, and the writing thus taken should be sent to the general recorder. Sands and Terry were by the Assembly appointed selectmen, and the freemen were to elect a third selectman. They were also to elect a clerk and constable, and to engage in the

2

colony's name to every officer elected, that the colony will stand by them in the discharge of their places and offices.

Judicial power up to forty shillings was given to the selectmen, and the Assembly intimate that if the people of the Island will bear the charge they may send two deputies to the General Assembly.

The Recorder was authorized to give the colony a copy of the laws for a small and equal consideration, and the Assembly judged it to be its duty to signify his majesty's most gracious pleasure vouchsafed in these words, viz: "That no person within the said colony at any time hereafter shall be in any way molested, punished, disquieted, or called in question for any difference of opinion in matters of religion, that do not actually disturb the civil peace of the said colony."

In 1664, the list of freemen was James Sands, Joseph Kent, Thomas Terry, Peter George, Simon Ray, William Harris, Samuel Dearing, John Rathbone, John Davis, Samuel Staples, Hugh Williams, Robert Guttory, William Tosh, Tormot Rose, William Cahoon, Tristam Dodge, John Clarke and William Barker. Hugh Williams had made some expressions inimical to the colony, which he was to retract before he could act as a freeman.

From 1663 to 1672, when the town was incorporated, the colonists appeared to be in some uncertainty as to whether they were rightfully a part of Massachusetts or of Rhode Island. They probably differed in opinion as to which colony they would prefer to belong; and during this period their government was a pure democracy, subject to no law superior to their own will. Then "it was ordered, that Joseph Billington plant and sufficiently tend three acres of Indian corn the next year ensuing, and so yearly during his abode here, and if he do not he shall depart the Island." It was also "ordered that the town's book shall be constantly kept in the hands of the town clerk, and a town clerk to be chosen yearly for that end who can both read and write."

A second plat of the Island was made by James Sands, Sen., John Rathbone, Sen., and John Williams.

There was evidently a party on the Island that favored the idea of their being within the Rhode Island Colony, and James Sands was the leader of this party.

At the May session of the General Assembly, 1665, the freemen of the Island elected Thomas Terry and James Sands to represent them in the General Assembly. The General Assembly, after a preamble and admonition, concluded to admit the members.

At the same session of the General Assembly, upon the petition of Thomas Terry, it was ordered that the governor, deputy governor and Mr. John Clarke take the pains to go to Block Island to see and judge whether there be a possibility to make a harbor, etc., and what conveniency there may be to give encouragement for a trade of fishing.

In May, 1670, Thomas Terry and Hugh Williams petitioned the General Assembly, that they might have the countenance of the government in proceeding to make a convenient harbor there. The General Assembly ordered that Caleb Carr and Joseph Torry of Newport, be desired and authorized to use their endeavors in persuading contributions and to keep an account, and to see that the money be improved to the matter intended, and not otherwise embezzled, provided that the harbor be free and common to all his majesty's liege people, as any other harbor in the colony is or shall be, without toll or impost.

The inhabitants of the Island were incorporated under a charter granted them, as the town of New Shoreham, at the October session of the General Assembly, 1672.

The town was authorized by the charter to elect a head-warden and a deputy-warden. These officers were to call town-meetings, to be magistrates, and with the other persons elected for that purpose, were to constitute the town council. The wardens when the exigency arose for a jury trial, had the power to procure a jury, to assist them in the administration of justice.

The town at the request and for the reasons assigned by the inhabitants, and as a sign of unity and likeness to many parts of our native country, was called New Shoreham, probably from Shoreham in the county of Sussex in England.

In 1678, the new comers were added to the list of freemen; and the entire list was recorded and embraced the following names, viz: James Sands, Simon Ray, Peter George, John Williams, Robert Guttory, John Sands, John Rathbone, Sen., Nathaniel Niles, James Sands, Jr., Thomas Mitchell, John Rathbone, Jr., Thomas Rathbone, Tristam Dodge, Jr., Samuel George, William Dodge, John Dodge, John Grinnal, Nathaniel Briggs, Daniel Tosh, Termot Rose, [illegible], Tristam Dodge, Sen., Edward Ball, John Ackers, William Frode, Benjamin Niles, and William Rathbone; 20th August, 1682, Nathaniel Winslow, Nathaniel Mott and John Mott were added to the list; Nathaniel Coddington was added in 1683; Josiah Holling, Joshua Billington, William Carder and William Hancock in 1684; James Danielson was there in 1685; Dr. John Rodman and Job Carr, both Quakers, were admitted, April 7th, 1690, and

Joshua Raymond, November 17th, of the same year. Many of these persons were not admitted free of the colony until long after they were free of the town. Richard Cozzens, though not a freeman, was at the Island in 1683, and Roger Kenyon also went there soon after.

CHAPTER II.

The Rev. Samuel Niles relates the following, viz: "I met with Captain James Babcock, late of Westerly, in Rhode Island government, not many miles distant from Ninicraft's fort, a gentleman of known fidelity and of uncommon generosity; and living near those Indians, was well acquainted with them and their manners. As we were together viewing the remains of Ninicraft's fort, he told me that in the time of Philip's war, as it was called in Plymouth and Massachusetts, Ninicraft was informed that three of his men were privately withdrawn, and had joined in the war against the English. Upon their return, Ninicraft cut off the feet of these men at their ancles, and then bid them run away to the war if they could. In that condition they crawled about until they died." This Babcock said the Indians told him. "At Block Island, where I was born, some time after the Island began to be settled by the English. there then being but sixteen Englishmen and a boy. and about three hundred Indians, the Indians were wont, some of them, to treat the English in a surly, lordly manner, which moved the English to suspect they had some evil designs in hand: and it being in the time of Philip's war, there was a large stone house garrisoned, erected by James Sands, Esq., one of the first settlers. To this garrison the women and children were gathered. But this was not esteemed a sufficient defence against such a great number of

Indians as were then on the Island. They therefore kept a very watchful eye on them, especially when they had got a considerable quantity of rum among them and they got drunk, as is common with them, and then they were ready for mischief. Once, when they had a large keg of rum, and it was feared by the English what might be the consequence, Mr. Thomas Terry, then an inhabitant there, the father of the present Colonel Terry, Esq., of Freetown, who had gained the Indian tongue, went to treat with them as they were gathered together on a hill that had a long descent to the bottom; where he found their keg or cask of rum, with the bung out, and began to inquire who had supplied them with it. They told him Mr. Arnold, who was a trader on Rhode Island. Upon which he endeavored to undervalue him and prejudice their minds against him; and in their cups they soon pretended that they cared as little for Mr. Arnold as he did. He told them, that if they spake the truth, they should prove it, which is customary among them, and the proof he directed was, to kick their keg of rum, and say, '*Tuckisba* Mr. Arnold;' the English is, 'I don't care for Mr. Arnold;' which one of them presently did, and with his kick rolled it down the hill, the bung being open, as was said; and by the time it came to the bottom, the rum had all run out. By this srategem, the English were made easy for this time.

"The Indians still insulting and threatening the English people, they became more cautious and watchful over them. About this time, or perhaps not long after, Ninicraft himself came over to visit this part of his dominions, as these islanders were his subjects, but his own seat was on the mainland over against them. And there came with him a number of his chief men, with many others, which gave the

English new grounds of suspicion, fearing what might be
their design, as they were drinking, dancing and revelling
after their usual customs at such times. Whereupon the
English went to parley with them, and to know what their
intentions were. The before mentioned James Sands, who
was the leading man among them, entered into a wigwam,
where he saw a very fine brass gun standing, and an Indian
fellow lying on a bench in the wigwam, probably to guard
and keep it. Mr. Sands's curiosity led him to take and
view it, as it made a curious and uncommon appearance.
Upon which the Indian fellow rises up hastily and snatches
the gun out of his hand, and withal gave such a violent
thrust with the butt end of it as occasioned him to stagger
backward. But feeling something under his feet, he espied
it to be a hoe, which he took up and improved, and with it
fell upon the Indian. Upon which a mighty scuffle ensued,
the English and Indians on the outside of the wigwam
closing in one with another; which probably would have
issued in the destruction of the whole English party, as they
were but a handful in comparison with the great number of
Indians, into whose hands they seemed then to have fallen,
had not God, by a remarkable instance of his power, prevented it. For, in the time of this tumult and impending
tragedy, Ninicraft, who was at that time on the Island, was
retired into a hot-house; there ran a messenger from the
company and acquainted him with the affair. Upon which
he came with all haste, and running into the wigwam, took
a scarlet colored coat, and brought it out, swinging it round
among the people as they were scuffling, and cries, 'King
Charles! King Charles!'—intimating thereby that as they
all were King Charles's subjects they ought not to contend;
which broke up the fray, and they became peaceable and

friendly together for that time. This coat and gun were likely sent by King Charles to Ninicraft, to engage his fidelity and friendship more strongly to the English.

"As I have mentioned the hot-house into which Ninicraft was at this time retired, it may not be amiss to acquaint my reader with the make, use, and design of the hot-houses among the aboriginal natives in this country, and perhaps in others also.

"They were made as a vault, partly under ground, and in the form of a large oven, where two or three persons might on occasion sit together, and it was placed near some depth of water: and their method was to heat some stones very hot in the fire, and put them into the hot-house, and when the person was in, to shut it close up, with only so much air as was necessary for respiration, or that they within might freely draw their breath. And being thus closely pent up, the heat of the stones occasioned them to sweat in a prodigious manner, streaming as it were from every part of the body; and when they had continued there as long as they could well endure it, their method was to rush out and plunge themselves into the water. By this means they pretend a cure of all pains and numbness in their joints, and many other maladies.

"Another instance of the remarkable interposition of Providence in the preservation of these few English people in the midst of a great company of Indians; the attempt was strange and not easily to be accounted for, and the event was as strange. The Indians renewing their insults, with threatening speeches, and offering smaller abuses, the English, fearing the consequences, resolved, these sixteen men and one boy, to make a formal challenge to fight this great company of Indians, near or full out three hundred, in

3

open pitched battle, and appointed the day for this effort.
Accordingly, when the day came, the before mentioned Mr.
Terry, living on a neck of land remote from the other English inhabitants, just as he was coming out of his house in
order to meet them, saw thirty Indians with their guns very
bright, as though they were fitted for war. He inquired
from whence they came. They replied, from Narragansett;
and that they were Ninicraft's men. He asked their business. They said, to see their relations and friends. And
for what reason they brought their guns? They replied,
because they knew not what game they might meet with in
their way. He told them that they must not carry their
guns any farther, but deliver them to him; and when they
returned, he would deliver them back to them safely. To
which they consented, and he secured them in his house, and
withal told them they must stay there until he had got past
the fort; as he was to go by it within gunshot over a narrow
beach between two ponds. The Indians accordingly all sat
down very quietly, but stayed not long after him; for he had
no sooner passed by the fort but the Indians made their
appearance on a hill, in a small neck of land called by the
English Indian-head-neck. And the reason of its being so
called was, because when the English came there, they found
two Indians' heads stuck upon poles standing there.—
Whether they were traitors or captives, I know not. When
they at the fort saw those thirty Indians that followed Mr.
Terry, they made a mighty shout; but Mr. Terry had, as I
observed, but just passed by it.

"However, the English, as few as they were, resolved to
pursue their design, and accordingly marched with their
drum beating up a challenge, (their drummer was Mr. Kent,
after of Swansey), and advanced within gunshot of it, as far

as the water would admit them, as it was on an island in a pond, near to and in plain sight of the place of my nativity. Thither they came with utmost resolution and warlike courage and magnanimity, standing the Indians to answer their challenge. Their drummer being a very active and sprightly man, and skilful in the business, that drum, under the overruling power of Providence, was the best piece of their armor. The Indians were dispirited to that degree that they made no motions against them. The English after inquired of them the reason of their refusing to fight with them, when they had so openly and near their fort made them such a challenge. They declared that the sound of the drum terrified them to that degree, that they were afraid to come against them. From this time the Indians became friendly to the English; and ever after. In this instance also God appeared for the defence of this small number of English people in their beginnings; for it was not the rattling, roaring sound of the drum, which doubtless they had heard before this time, but Divine sovereignty made this a means to intimidate them, and restrain their cruel and barbarous dispositions."

CHAPTER III.

"Some time in July, 1689, three French privateer vessels came to Block Island; upon which the people were alarmed, not then knowing whether they were English or French. The vessels were a large barque, a barge, a large sloop, and a lesser one. They had an Englishman with them, one William Trimming, who was wont treacherously to decoy and betray those they met with at sea, pretending they were Englishmen, as he had the perfect use of the English tongue. Him they sent on shore with some men in a perianger, which lay off at a small distance; whilst he took the advantage of stepping from one rock to another, and came alone to the islanders who were standing on the shore in arms; who inquired of him who they were, and from whence they came, and whither they were bound, and their captain, or commodore's name. To which he answered, their commodore was George Astin, (of whom they had often heard as a noted privateer, that had done great exploits against the French and Spaniards in the West Indies), and that they were Englishmen,—when they were a mixed company, mostly French, with some Spaniards and Mestizos, and their Captain's name was Pekar, a Frenchman; that they came from Jamaica, and were bound into Newport on Rhode Island, (which was so far true, that their design was to take and rifle that town), that they wanted a pilot to conduct

them into the harbor, and that they wanted to be supplied
with some wood and water, and fresh provisions for their
money. This was a plausible and very pleasing account to
the inhabitants, though perfidiously false in the articles of
greatest importance. What farther confirmed their credit in
the case was, there happened to be a stranger on the island
at that time, and then among the people, who pretended a
particular acquaintance with Captain Astin, and also sent
his compliments to him; so that, upon the whole, the
islanders were very well satisfied, and fearless of danger.
Upon having thus told his story, Trimming, doubtless much
pleased, went off to the periauger that waited for him. He
having made a motion for a pilot to Newport, which was
about ten leagues distant from them, several that had sailed
to and from thence, in hopes of some great reward, went on
board. They no sooner were got there, but they were immediately clapped down under the hatches, and examined
on the strength of Newport, and of Block Island; and finding this last not able to resist them, they resolved to play
their game in plundering the people of this island. Accordingly, manning their three periaugers with about 50
men in each of them, they made to the harbor, having their
guns all lying in the bottom of their boats out of sight;
where the people met them, and were something amused
at their great number. But being well satisfied, as they
thought, there was no monkery in the case, therefore in a
very friendly manner directed them to shun some sunken
rocks that lay at the entrance into the harbor; and to re-
quite their kindness, as they laid to the wharf, every one of
them started up with his gun presented, and told the people
if they stirred from the place, or made resistance, they
were dead men. Thus tamely and unexpectedly, to their

great surprise, they were all taken and made prisoners of
war. As for their coming in such great numbers, as before
is noted, which at first gave the people some grounds of suspicion, to this they were soon reconciled, supposing that
they were willing to walk and divert themselves on the land,
as they had been a long time at sea. So that all circumstances seemed to concur, by the treachery of this Trimming, to
make them an easy prey to their enemies.

"As they were thus become masters of the island, they disarmed the men, and stove their guns to pieces on the rocks,
and carried the people and confined them in the house of
Captain James Sands, before mentioned, which was large and
accommodable for their purpose, and not far from the harbor.
This they made their prison, and place of rendezvous, and
soon set upon plundering houses, and killing cattle, sheep
and hogs, some to feed on, others for waste and spoil, and to
impoverish the inhabitants. One instance among others,
was their shooting a large cow that had a very full bag, and
the rather as she had not been milked for some time ; and
for no other reason, as was said, than to cut off her bag and
carry on board their vessel to suck the milk out of her teats,
leaving her to rot on the ground, as they did many other
creatures.

"However, news quickly reached to the main, that Block
Island was taken by the French; upon which the country
was alarmed, and bonfires made from Pawcatuck Point,
which is the utmost extent of Rhode Island government
next to Connecticut, and from thence round on Rhode Island
to Seconet Point, which then was the farthest part of the
Massachusetts government, but is now taken into the government of Rhode Island, upon a late overture of that affair;
whether justly or not it is neither my province nor purpose

now to determine. They continued about a week on the island, plundering houses, stripping the people of their clothing, ripping up beds, throwing out the feathers, and carrying away the ticking.

" In this time they offered great abuses to Simon Ray, Esq., an aged gentleman, who lived somewhat remote in the island, and had not removed his money nor choicest part of his goods out of his house until they saw a company of the enemy at a distance coming thither. He and his son, (who was of the same name, and after bore the like distinguishing characters of honor and usefulness that his father had done before, who is now lately deceased also), as there was no minister in the place, were wont, in succession, in a truly Christian, laudable manner, to keep a meeting in their own house on Lord's days, to pray, sing a suitable portion of the Psalms, and read in good sermon books, and as they found occasion, to let drop some words of exhortation in a religious manner on such as attended their meeting. Upon the sight of the French coming, the son (then a young man) with the servants carried out some chests and what they could most readily convey out of the house, and hid them, and themselves also. When the Frenchmen came into the house, they found only the old gentleman and his wife ; all the rest of the family were fled. The Frenchmen demanded his money. He told them he had none at his command. They observing, by the signs on the floor, that chests and other things were lately removed, and the money which they principally aimed at, asked him where they were. He told them he did not know, for his people had carried them out, and he could not tell where they put them. They bid him call his folks, that they might bring them again ; which he did, but had no answer, for they were all fled out of hearing. They being thus disappointed, one of them in a violent rage, got a piece of a rail, and struck him on his head therewith, and in such fury that the blood instantly gushed out and ran on the floor. Upon which his wife took courage, and sharply reprehended them for killing her husband, which she then supposed they had done. Upon this they went off, without the game they expected. After the flow of blood was over, he recovered his health, and lived many years in his former religious usefulness, as before is noted.

"Another man they used barbarously, by tricing him up and whipping him in an unmerciful manner, to make him confess where his money was, and bring it to them; when at the same time, as he declared to them, he had none or next to none. The case was this, (as I understood it). They inquired of some one or more of the people, Who were the likeliest among them to have money? They told them of John Rathbun, who was the most likely. This poor man bearing his father's name, (they supposing him to be the person), suffered this cruelty in the room of his father, who escaped by that means with his money.

"In the time of these privateers' stay on the Island, they killed two negro men, one belonging to the above mentioned Mr. Ray, if I mistake not, and the other to Captain John Sands, who is also mentioned before: and two other negro fellows ran from their master, and voluntarily resigned themselves to the French, of whom there was no further account what became of them. They were Dr. John Rodman's servants. He was a gentleman of great ingenuity, and of an affable, engaging behavior, of the profession of them called Quakers. He also kept a meeting in his house on the Sabbaths, with exhortations unto good works, after the manner of the teachers in that society, but more agreeably than I suppose is common with them, whose meetings I had attended often in my younger time. It was said of him, when these Frenchmen came to his house, one of them essayed to lead his wife (who was also a very desirable gentlewoman) into a private room, but Mr. Rodman stepped into the doorway and prevented him; upon which the ruffian cocked his pistol, threatening to shoot him. He opened his clothes on his breast, replying, 'Thee mayst do it if thou pleasest, but thou shalt not abuse my wife.' While they remained riding in the bay they took two vessels bound up the Sound, one laden with steel mostly, which they sunk; the other was laden with wine and spirituous liquors, which they purposed to carry off with them, but they were prevented, as we shall find afterwards.

"The privateers perceiving, by the bonfires before spoken of, that the country was alarmed, and perhaps, by those that had gone on board them with hopes of becoming their pilots, before mentioned, being informed of the strength and numbers of men on Rhode Island, were discouraged making an attempt on Newport; therefore determined to attack New London. Accordingly they sailed thither, and up into the harbor. The country being before alarmed, as was said, and having had intelligence of their approach, the men in the bordering towns came down in great numbers; and the fort with their great guns firing on them, they found the harbor too hot for them. They therefore drew off, and concluded to return to Block Island, and renew their spoils and plunder there. Some of their company went on an Island called Fisher's Island, lying near New London, and among others this treacherous fellow. Trimming, before spoken of, of which they had some intelligence at Stonington. Upon which 17 men went from thence over to the island, which

4

is not far distant in the easternmost end. There was but
one house on the island, though about nine miles in length,
where this party of Frenchmen were at that time. The
English got near the house before they were discovered;
upon which Trimming came out to them, in a pretended
friendly manner, drawing his gun behind him. They demanded who and from whence they were. He replied, they
were cast-away men. One of the Englishmen replied, 'If
you are friends, lay down your gun, and come behind us.'
Immediately Mr. Stephen Richardson, as was supposed
through surprise, shot him dead on the spot, for which act
he was much blamed.' Thus he that delighted in falsehood
in his life, died with a lie in his mouth, and received, it
seems, the just reward of his perfidious, villanous and multi-
plied treacheries.

"Whilst these French privateers were making an attempt
at New London, the people of Newport fitted out two vessels
from thence with volunteers to engage them, supposing they
were still at Block Island. These vessels were sloops, under the command of Captain and Commodore Paine, who
had some years before followed the privateering design, and
Captain John Godfrey, his second; and inquiring for the
French, they were told, that when they left the island they
shaped their course westward toward New London; upon
which our English vessels streched off to the southward,
and soon made a discovery of a small fleet standing eastward. Supposing them to be the French they were in quest
of, they tacked and came in as near shore as they could
with safety, carrying one anchor to wear and another to
seaboard, to prevent the French boarding them on each side
at once, and to bring their guns and men all on one side, the
better to defend themselves and annoy the enemy. The

French probably discovered them also, and made all the sail they could, expecting to make prizes of them. Accordingly they sent a periauger before them, full of men, with design to pour in their small arms on them, and take them, as their manner was, supposing they were unarmed vessels and only bound upon trade. Captain Paine's gunner urged to fire on them. The Captain denied, alleging it more advisable to let the enemy come nearer under their command. But the gunner still urging it, being certain (as he said) he should rake fore and aft, thus with much importunity at length the Captain gave him liberty. He fired on them but the bullet went wide of them, and I saw it skip on the surface of the water several times, and finally lodged in a bank, as they were not very far distant from the shore. This brought them to a stand, and to row off as fast as they could and wait until their vessels came up. When they came, they bore down on the English, and there ensued a very hot sea-fight for several hours, though under the land, the great barque foremost, pouring in a broadside with small arms. Ours bravely answered them in the same manner, with their huzzas and shouting. Then followed the larger sloop, the captain whereof was a very violent, resolute fellow. He took a glass of wine to drink, and wished it might be his damnation if he did not board them immediately. But as he was drinking, a bullet struck him in his neck, with which he instantly fell down dead, as the prisoners (before spoken of) afterward reported. However, the large sloop proceeded, as the foremost vessel had done, and the lesser sloop likewise. Thus they passed by in course, and then tacked and brought their other broadside to bear. In this manner they continued the fight until the night came on and prevented their farther conflict. Our men as valiantly paid

them back in their own coin, and bravely repulsed them,
and killed several of them. The Captain, before spoken of,
with one or more were after driven on the shore. In this
action the continued fire was so sharp and violent, that the
echo in the woods made a noise as though the limbs of the
trees were rent and tore off from their bodies (as I have
observed); yet they killed but one man, an Indian fellow of
the English party, and wounded six men, who after recovered. They overshot our men, so that many of their bullets,
both great and small, were picked up on the adjacent shore.

Our men expected a second encounter in the morning,
and their ammunition being much spent, sent in the night
for the island's stock, as the French lay off at anchor but a
small distance from them all night. But having found the
engagement too hot for them, they hoisted their sails and
stood off to sea; and one reason might be this (as was
reported) that their Commodore understood by some means
that it was Captain Paine he had encountered, said, 'He
would as soon choose to fight with the devil as with him.'
Such was their dialect. Now this Captain Paine, and Peckar
the French Commodore, had sailed together a privateering,
Paine captain, and Peckar his lieutenant, in some former
wars. The French standing off to sea, Captain Paine and
Captain Godfrey, and their soldiers, with the valor and
spirit of true Englishmen, pursued them, but the privateers
being choice sailors, were too light of foot for them. The
French, finding that they hauled on the vessel before spoken
of, loaded with wines and brandy, which was not so good a
sailor as the others, and fearing the English would make a
prey of her, fired a great shot through her bottom, so that
when our men came to her she was sunk under water in her

fore part, the stern alone buoyed up by a long-boat fastened to it; and as she was standing right up and down in the water, they could not get anything out of her. They no sooner cut the painter, but she instantly sunk to the bottom. They brought the boat with them in their return, which was the only prize and trophy of their victory; only as the enemy were vanquished, and that they had so courageously chased them off the New England coast. When Peckar heard that Trimming was killed, he greatly lamented, and said, he had rather have lost thirty of his men.

Before the year was expired, some of the same company, with others, landed in the night, and surprised the people in their beds, and proceeded in like mannor as before, plundering houses, stripping the people of their clothing, killing creatures and making great waste and spoil; but killed no person. I suppose I was the greatest sufferer of any under their hands at this time; for before I had dressed myself, one of their company rushed into the chamber where I lodged. After some free and seemingly familiar questions he asked me, which I answered with like freedom; but being alone, without any of his company, not knowing what danger might befall him (as I after apprehended)—on a sudden and with a different air, he says to me, 'Go down, you dog.' To which I replied, 'Presently; as soon as I have put on my stockings and shoes.' At which with the muzzle of his gun he gave such a violent thrust at the pit of my stomach, that it threw me backwards on the bed, as I was sitting on the bed side, so that it was some time before I could recover my breath. As soon as I could, I gathered them up. He drew his cutlass and beat me, smiting with all his power, to the head of the stairs, and it was a very large chamber. He followed me down the stairs, and then bound my hands behind me with a sharp small line, which soon made my hands swell and become painful. How I managed after with my stockings and shoes, I have now forgot. However, after this I met with no abuse from them the whole time of their stay on the island.

"The first time the island was taken, of which I have given a narrative before, I took the first opportunity to make my escape, and some others did the like; and though we camped in a small piece of upland in a great swamp, yet every leaf that stirred with the wind, made me with surprise conclude the French were come upon us. This made me determine with myself, that if ever it were my lot in providence to be taken by them again, I would continue in and see the worst of my bondage, until it pleased God to send me deliverance. This resolution I held, though I had a fair opportunity to make an escape, and notwithstanding the ill treatment I met with at first, as before related.

"The French came a third time while I was on the island, and came to anchor in the bay on Saturday, some time before night; and acquainted us who they were and what they intended, by hoisting up their white colors. None of the people appearing to oppose them, and having, at this time, my aged grand-parents, Mr. James Sands and his wife, before mentioned, to take the care of, with whom I then dwelt; knowing also, that if they landed they would make his house the chief seat of their rendezvous, as they had done twice before, and not knowing what insults or outrage they might commit on them, I advised to the leaving their house, and betaking themselves to the woods for shelter, till they might return under prospects of safety; which they consented to. Accordingly we took our flight into the woods, which were at a considerable distance, where we encamped that night as well as the place and circumstances would allow, with some others, that for the like reasons fell into our company. The next morning, being the Lord's day morning, I expressed my desire to go occultly and see the conduct of the French, and their proceedings. One of the company offered to go with me. We went together, and placed ourselves on the top of a hill, where were small bushes and a large swamp behind us, but in fair sight of the house I went from. viz: my grandfather's house. It seems the French had not landed until that morning, for we had not long been seated there before we saw them coming from the water-side in two files. which made a long train, with their colors flying, and, if I mistake not, their trumpet sounding. (I did not then think of counting their number.) Thus they came in triumph, and as absolute lords of the soil and all belonging thereto,—as indeed they were for the time; but their reign was but short, as the sequel will prove. (My companion in this discovery was Mr. Thomas Mitchell, who then, and many years after, was an inhabitant on Block Island, alias New Shoreham.) In this manner they went to the house, and immediately set up their standard on a hill on the back side of it, and directly shot and killed three hogs fatted with whey in a sty, and then killed the geese, as there were many there. Having had but little sleep the night before, I proposed to Mr. Mitchell to keep a good look-out, and watch their motions, till I endeavored to sleep a little, and thus to proceed interchangeably: when I made the hard ground my lodging for the time. which was long. Upon my awaking, he lay down ; and as he lay and slept, the French fired many guns at the house, and I heard several bullets whistling over my head. Suspecting they had made

some discovery of us, I awakened him, telling him what I
had observed; therefore that it was advisable to shift our
quarters. Accordingly, as we were moving from the place,
we espied a large ship about a league to leeward of the
township, riding at anchor, (the fog at sea had been very
thick till then), which happened to be Captain Dobbins, in
the Nonesuch man-of-war, stationed in those seas, which we
at first sight supposed. This ship appearing, put the Frenchmen into a great surprise, by their motions, by running up
to their standard on the hill, then down again, and others
doing the like. The man-of-war still making all sail possible, there being but a small breeze of wind at southwest,
and right ahead, according to the sailors' phrase, they soon
left the house, and with all speed and seeming confusion
hastened to their vessel. Upon this, we went boldly to the
house, and found the floor covered with geese, with blood,
and feathers; the quarters of the hogs they had killed hang-
ing up in one and another part of the house,—a melancholy
sight to behold. Their manner of dressing hogs after they
had quartered them, was to singe off the hair over a flame;
and their method to command the cattle was (as I saw when
they took us before) to thrust their cutlasses in at their loins,
and on a sudden the hind quarter would fall down, and as
the poor creature strove to go forward, the blood would
spout out of the hole, and fly up near or full out a yard in
height. But to return.—the Frenchmen hastened on board,
as they had taken many prisoners in their passage, and
among others, one Captain Rodney, with his lady, a gentleman of a fine estate, coming from the West Indies, with all
his substance, to settle in this country. They robbed him of
all his wealth, insomuch, as in my hearing his wife related,
that when they saw they were likely to be taken, she took a

bag of money and hid it in a private place. However, they found it, and took it from her. These prisoners, they used the utmost dexterity to set on shore, and leave behind them; which they no sooner had done but they set sail to make their escape, the Nonesuch all this while pressing hard to windward. Soon after these privateers took to their heels, hoping to get out of the man-of-war's reach, the fog thickened, and the wind rose and blew hard at southwest, so that we quickly lost sight of them both. The French kept close upon the wind, in hopes to weather a place called Noman's Land, lying southward of Martha's Vineyard; but the wind scanting on them, and blowing hard, they ran into a place (if I mistake not) called Buzzard's Bay, which emphatically proved so to them. There they were land-locked, and could not get out, although the French vessel was quickly out of sight by reason of the thick fog which continued. Yet as if the Nonesuch had tracked them by the print of their heels in the ocean, or had followed them in their wake, she came in upon them, Providence so ordering, and took them. When they saw, to their astonishment, the man-of-war so unexpectedly overtaking them, about 40 of their men went on shore and were disarmed and seized by the people that dwelt near the place, and sent prisoners to Boston. The others on board, Captain Dobbins took and made prisoners of war, and their ship became a rich prize, which we saw about three days after, following him into Newport, where she was condemned.

"These French privateers, or some others, came a fourth time, and landed on Block Island, in the former war with France; but the people on the island took courage, and encountered them in an open pitched battle, and drove them

5

off from the shore, without any hurt to the English, except
one man slightly wounded in his finger. They never after
that troubled the people any more."

"The great spoil made on the island by the French, in
their repeated visits, and particularly on my father's interest,
occasioned my staying from school six years (when I intended only a short visit to my friends.) In this time I turned
my hand to husbandry, and sometimes to handicraft. I
helped to build a vessel, among other things, for the West
India trade; and caulked one side and the master-workman
the other; and she proved very tight, and answerable to the
design. After the space of six years thus employed, I returned again to school, so that, by reason of this delay, I
was near two-and-twenty years old when I entered into the
College at Cambridge, the reverend Dr. Increase Mather
then being President,—and Mr. John Leverett, afterward
President, and Mr. William Brattle, after the reverend pas-
tor of Cambridge church, were the only fellows. The
kindness of these worthy gentlemen I hope not to forget,
who, I conclude, favored me the more, as I was the first that
came to college from Rhode Island government.

    *   *   *   *   *

"June 1, 1706, Mr. Walker, being laden with provisions
from Connecticut, was chased by a French privateer. To
shun being taken by him, he ran ashore in his boat, and as
he hastened to Rhode Island, alarmed the country round
about. The people there were so expeditious, that in a few
hours, (by beat of the drum) 100 men well equipped, voluntarily entered on board two sloops, under the command of
Major Wanton (after Governor there, and Captain Paine,
the same famous old warrior that, with Captain Godfrey (as

before is related) put to flight the French fleet of privateers from Block Island. The very next day they made a prize of her, wherein were 37 men under the command of Captain Ferrel, bound for Port Royal, as it was called while in the hands of the French, but now Annapolis."

At a special session of the General Assembly held September 16th, 1690, the Assembly voted to pay the charges of the expedition of Captain Thomas Paine, and Captain Godfrey against the enemy, to Block Island.

The colony afterwards sent soldiers to Block Island, who were supported by the inhabitants of the Island, and pai by the colony, and the people of the Island were much of the time obliged to keep watch and ward, as their records abundantly show from 1689 to subsequent to 1740.

The affair referred to by Niles as having taken place in 1706, is more in detail referred to by Weston Clarke, Secretary of the colony in a letter in behalf of the Governor and Council of Rhode Island, to the Board of Trade. This letter is dated September 14th, which is as follows, viz : "About two months since an express being sent to the Governor. that a French privateer had taken a trading sloop laden with provisions, upon the coast, the evening before the express came, the Governor upon the receipt of the news immediately caused proclamation to be made for volunteers, as is our custom in such cases to go against her majesty's enemies; and in two hours time had two sloops, which he had taken up for said service, fitted and manned with one hundred and twenty men, who within three hours after, upon the coast of Block Island, made themselves masters of said French privateer, and the prize she had taken, and brought them into this port, (Newport.)"

The General Assembly passed an act in 1708, in consequence of a petition from the men of the Island that they were in great danger from the French, to send fifteen men, English and Indians, to be kept at the Island as long, and to be abated, as the Governor, Assistant and Major of the Island should see cause.

In the Spring of 1740, ten men were directed to be impressed from the King's County, and ten from the county of Providence, to be sent to the Island for six months for its defence ; the men to be billeted among the inhabitants ; the six guns at the Island were to be mounted, and provision was made for a supply of ammunition and gun carriages.

CHAPTER IV

THE PALATINE SHIP.

The upper and lower Palatinate were two separate states of ancient Germany. The upper Palatinate embraced what is now known as Bavaria, and the lower Palatinate a territory on both sides of the Rhine, within which were the cities of Mannheim and Heidleberg. The area of the latter territory was about sixteen hundred square miles, and the former contained twenty-seven hundred and thirty square miles. James I, after his disastrous attempt to succor the unfortunate Palatines, upon his death bed, in 1625, exhorted Charles I, to bear a tender affection for his (James) wife, to preserve a constancy in religion, to protect the Church of England, and to extend his care towards the unhappy families of the Palatines.

It was natural that Protestant England should be interested in these persecuted Christians.

While Marlborough was operating with the allied armies in that country, ten thousand of this distressed people had been invited to England. They were graciously received by Queen Anne. They had been preceded in 1708, by a party of fifty, who had been commended to the Queen by the chaplain of Prince George. The Queen had allowed them a shilling a day and had charged herself with the burden of their transportation to the colonies. The favor they had received, was told of in the letters written home to their impoverished countrymen. The Anabaptists of Holland aided the Palatines in emigrating to England, and to the plantations in America.

Those who went to England arrived in a season of scarcity, and though great charities were set on foot to aid them, their arrival produced much discontent among the English poor. Many of the Palatines were sent to Ireland, but most of them to North America.

At the beginning of the eighteenth century and during its first quarter, the section of New York from Lake Champlain to Lake Erie extending south below the Mohawk valley, was a wilderness. The French then hostile to the English, possessed Canada. The inhabitants of the lower Palatinate had been the subjects of persecution by the French during the religious wars of Europe, for one hundred years. Under the patronage of the Queen large bodies of these Palatines were sent to New York, and were settled on the banks of the Hudson and in the northern section of New York, to form a barrier between the older population of that country and the French in Canada Two of these bodies of emigrants came by the way of England, and the third came, in 1722, from Holland. The first two bodies arrived, one in 1708, and the other in 1710. It would be interesting to trace the history of these emigrants in building up the great States of New York and Pennsylvania, but that is aside from our present purpose.

"The Palatine," "The Phantom Ship," immortalized by Dana's Buccaneers, and Whittier's little poem, as associated with the history of Block Island and its vicinity, is the subject we are to consider.

That there was a ship freighted with Palatine emigrants bound for New York or Pennsylvania, that came to this country and with which was associated some great crime or disaster which occurred in the vicinity of Block Island, is true beyond question, if we are to regard evidence to establish any fact which did not arise within our own personal cognizance.

There are now living many persons who have seen and conversed with many persons who had seen and conversed with at least two of the survivors of the emigrants that came in this ship.

On the south side of Block Island, but a few rods to the west of where the Ann Hope, the India ship of Brown & Ives, was wrecked, and some forty or fifty rods to the east of "The Black Rock Gully" on a little knoll, is a cluster of graves; up to within a few years, they were distinctly visible, but the unfeeling plow has passed over them, and has almost obliterated their existence.

In "the Pocock meadow," a mile further westward, and in a field lately owned by the late Jesse Lewis, were other clusters of graves, long within my memory, if not now, clearly visible. These were all known as "the Palatine graves." The existence of these graves and their designation will not be questioned.

The traditional story is, that "the Palatine"—for want of the real name of the ship I adopt the name by which she has been designated,—sailed from Holland about 1720. That she was ladened with emigrants and their effects. That though most of the emigrants were poor, they were not all so.

That the passengers on the voyage were nearly starved.
That the ship lingered about Block Island for a considerable
time, and after many of the passengers had died, the survivors, with the exception of a lady of great wealth, who refused to leave the ship, were landed on the Island. That one
man from the island, Mark Dodge, was frequently on board
the ship, and was intimate with the officers. Some of the
passengers were taken into the house of a Mr. Ray, a de-
scendant of Simon Ray, and were there cared for. That they
had been so long deprived of food, and eat so voraciously in
their then diseased condition, that they all died but three
women. The officers of the ship took the treasure and
abandoned the ship.

Two of the survivors of this ship lived and died on the
Island. They were respectively known as "Tall Kattern"
and "Short Kattern." These poor women were young, des-
titute, and though apparently well bred, at least this was the
case with Short Kattern, they were ignorant of the language
of the people with whom their lot was cast. Tall Kattern
formed some connexion with an African negro, who had been
imported into the colony and purchased at the Island and
who was called New Port, after the town from which he
came. They had at least three children, viz : Thomas Port,
Mary Port, and Kreadle Port. Mille Babcock, who died at
the Newport Asylum within the last year, who was said to have
been in the one hundred and second year of her age, was
the grand-daughter of Thomas Port, and the great grand-
daughter of Tall Kattern. Short Kattern was supported by
the town, that is, she was billeted about among the inhabitants, and died there, and is said to have been buried in the
corner of a private burying ground, lately belonging to the
late Josiah S. Peckham.

I very well remember Kreadle, the daughter of Tall Kattern; she probably died about 1828 or 29, aged about 100 years. There is a tradition that there was a third survivor who married in Washington county and left descendants, but this I have not had the time to investigate.

Mark Dodge was insane for years, but even in his maniacal ravings no one could ever elicit anything from him about what took place on board the Palatine. The asking of this simple question would calm his rage and induce his silence. The rest of the story others must tell.

The appearance of Whittier's Poem, "The Palatine," has revived the interest which formerly existed in the legend which is its subject, and which was the subject of the justly celebrated poem of Dana, called "The Bucaneers."

Mr. Bull says he obtained the traditionary story of the ship from William P. Sands, an inhabitant of Block Island, and that Mr. Sands obtained it from a very reputable lady who was an aunt of his.

Mr. Sands was a well known citizen of the Island, represented the town in the General Assembly for several years, was a man of intelligence and of high character for probity ; he died at an advanced age about thirty years since.

He said that the tradition in relation to the Palatine was, "that she was run on shore on Block Island, about the year 1719 or 1720, but a northeast gale and high tide floated her off after lying several days. She was from Holland, bound to Pennsylvania with emigrants. Having a long passage, and being put on short allowance, most of the emigrants died from hardships and disease, arising, as they believed, principally from the desire of the captain to appropriate their effects to his own use. The surviving passengers, 16 or 17 in

6

number, were landed, but in so diseased a state that three
only survived, who remained and became inhabitants of the
island. One lady passenger [Mary Vanderline] who had much
gold and silver plate on board, refused to quit the ship; she
remained on board and must have perished, as the ship was
never after heard of. One year after which, the Palatine light,
as it is called, appeared in the offing, and has continued occa-
sionally to appear up to the year 1832, since which it has not
been observed. Some of the silver cups which belonged to
the passengers are still to be seen on the Island."

The following account of the Palatine light is taken
from a publication called the Parthenon. It was written
by Dr. Aaron C. Willey, a resident physician of the Island,
to Dr. Samuel L. Mitchell, of New York. :

BLOCK ISLAND, Dec. 10, 1811.

DEAR SIR :—In a former letter I promised to give you an
account of the singular light which is sometimes seen from
this place. I now hasten to fulfil my engagement. I should
long since have communicated the fact to the literary world,
but was unwilling to depend wholly upon the information of
others, when by a little delay, there was probability of my
receiving occular demonstration. I have not, however, been
so fortunate in this respect as I could wish, having had only
two opportunities of viewing the phenomenon. My residing
nearly six miles from the shore, which lies next to the
region of its exhibition and behind elevated ground, has prevented me from seeing it so frequently, perhaps, as I might
otherwise have done. The people who have always lived
here are so familiarized to the sight that they never think of
giving notice to those who do not happen to be present, or
even of mentioning it afterwards, unless they hear some
particular enquiries are made.

This curious irradiation rises from the ocean near the northern part of the island. Its appearance is nothing different from a blaze of fire; whether it actually touches the water, or merely hovers over it, is uncertain, for I am informed that no person has been near enough to decide accurately. It beams with various magnitudes, and appears to bear no more analogy to the *ignus fatuus* than it does to the aurora borealis. Sometimes it is small, resembling the light through a distant window; at others expanding to the highness of a ship with all her canvass spread. When large, it displays either a pyramidical form, or three constant streams. In the latter case, the streams are somewhat blended together at the bottom, but separate and distinct at the top, while the middle one rises rather higher than the other two. It may have the same appearance when small, but owing to distance and surrounding vapors, cannot be clearly perceived. This light often seems to be in a constant state of mutation; decreasing by degrees it becomes invisible, or resembles a lucid point then shining anew, sometimes with a sudden flare, at others by a gradual increasement to its former size. Often the mutability regards the lustre only, becoming less and less bright until it disappears or nothing but a pale outline can be discerned of its full size, then resuming its full splendor, in the manner before related. The duration of its greatest and least state of illumination is not commonly more than three minutes; this inconstancy, however, does not appear in every instance.

After the radiance seems to be totally extinct, it does not always return in the same place, but is not unfrequently seen shining at some inconsiderable distance from which it disappeared. In this transfer of locality it seems to have no certain line of direction.

When most expanded, this blaze is generally wavering like the flame of a torch. At one time it appears stationary, at another progressive. It is seen at all seasons of the year, and for the most part in the calm weather which precedes an easterly or southerly storm. It has, however, been noticed during a severe northwestern gale, and when no storm immediately followed. Its continuance is sometimes but transient, at others throughout the night, and it has been known to appear several nights in succession.

This blaze actually emits luminous rays. A gentleman whose house is situated near the sea, informs me that he has known it to illuminate considerably the walls of his room through the windows. This happens only when the light is within half a mile of the shore; for it is often seen blazing at six or seven miles distance, and strangers suppose it to be a vessel on fire.

Having given a concise but general description of this unusual radiance, in which I have been aided by the concurrent testimony of diverse veritable characters, I will now offer you those observations afforded me by the opportunities I have had for visiting it myself. The first time I beheld it was at evening twilight, in February, 1810. It was large and gently lambent, very bright, broad at the bottom and terminating acutely upward. From each side seemed to issue rays of faint light, similar to those perceptible in any blaze placed in the open air at night. It continued about fifteen minutes from the time I first observed it; then gradually became smaller until more dim, and it was entirely extinguished.

I saw it again on the evening of December the 20th. It was then small, and I supposed it to be a light on board of some vessel, but I was soon undeceived. It moved along, apparently parallel to the shore, for about two miles, in the time that I was riding one at a moderate pace. An ascent of ground then hid it for a few minutes from my view. Passing this I observed it about half way back to the place where it had commenced its vagrant career. I then stopped to observe it more attentively. The light then remained still for some time—them moved off quickly for several rods, and made a halt; thus being in a state of alternate motion and rest. Its magnitude and lustre were subject to the same unsteadiness described above.

This lucid meteor has long been known by the name of the Palatine light. By the ignorant and superstitious, it is thought to be supernatural. Its appellation originated from that of a a ship called the Palatine, which was designedly cast away at this place, in the beginning of the last century, in order to conceal, as tradition reports, the inhuman treatment and murder of some of its unfortunate passengers. From this time, it is said, the Palatine light appeared, and there are many who firmly believe it to be a ship on fire, to which their fantastic and distempered imaginations figure masts, ropes and flowing sails.

The cause of this "roving brightness" is a curious subject for philosophical investigation. Some, perhaps, will suppose it will depend upon a peculiar modification of electricity; others upon the inflammation of phlogogistous (hydrogenous) gas. But there are, possibly, many other means, unknown to us, by which light may be devolved from those materials with which it is latently associated, by the power of mechanical affinities.

I have stated to you facts, but feel a reluctance to **hazard** any speculation. These I leave to you and to other acute researchers of created ·things. Your opinion I would be much pleased with.

I remain yours, &c.,

AARON C. WILLEY.

HON. S. L. MITCHELL.

CHAPTER V.

Much of the town records from the foundation of the colony up to the breaking out of the revolution is taken up in matters appertaining to defence, to provisions for arms and amunition, for watch and ward, for modes of alarm, and in the event of an alarm what was to be done. The mind wearies with these details as it tries to compass the history of this people.

Other colonists may have been subjected to even greater hardships, or may have endured them more heroically than these, but taking into consideration all of the circumstances which surrounded them, the people of this island have produced creditable results. The schoolmaster has not long been abroad there.

During the wars between France and England, it was often found to be impracticable for the colony to defend the inhabitants of this island from the marauding cruisers of the French; they at these unguarded times pounced upon the inhabitants and committed such depredations upon their property as they chose with impunity, and upon the breaking out of the revolution, the colony could not defend the Island, and it is repeatedly referred to in the Colonial Records as being in the possession of the enemy. The inhabitants of the Island were greatly impoverished during this war; a considerable number of the able bodied men left the colony to engage in the service of their country, either on board of privateers or in the army, and the removal by the colony of a large number of cattle and sheep, and the prohibiting the inhabitants of the Island to go to the main land, or people from the main land to go to the Island except by the special authority of the General Assembly, isolated these people in a way that it was impossible for them to obtain from external sources any of the comforts or conveniences of life. They were dependent for their clothing upon the wool they grew from the few sheep that were left them, and the flax they raised, both of which were made into cloth by the women of that time. The enemy took from them what they pleased, and paid for what they took according to their pleasure. The officers generally paid for what they had, but the men, probably, did not.

The stories of the privations and sufferings of this people during the eight years of the war, may have been exaggerations of facts as they occurred, for the adversities in youth appear to the aged to have been greater than they were, as when we return to the old country homestead after a long absence in the city, we are disappointed at the smallness of its dimensions.

At a town meeting, held March 2d, 1774, John Sands, Esq., was chosen moderator.

They resolved that the Americans had as good right to be free as any people on earth ; that the right claimed by Parliament to bind the colonies in all cases whatever, is inconsistent with the natural, constitutional and chartered rights and privileges of this colony ; that a tax levied on Americans for the support of government, has a tendency to render colonial assemblies useless, and to introduce arbitrary government and slavery; that the taxation of a people without their consent, is destructive of freedom; that the attempt of the East India Company to force their tea into America, subject to a duty here, is a violent attack upon the liberties of the country, and it is the duty of every American to oppose this attempt; that every individual who countenances this attempt, or who in any way aids it, or pilots any vessel with tea on board, is an enemy to his country, and that they would heartily unite with their brethren of the colony in supporting the inhabitants of this continent in all their just rights and privileges, and that Joshua Sands, Caleb Littlefield and John Sands, Esquires, and Messrs. Walter Rathbone and Edward Sands, Jr., be a committee of the town to correspond with all of the committees of the towns of the colony, and the said committee is requested to give the closest attention to everything which concerns the liberties of America. At this time the population of the Island was 575, of whom 51 were Indians and 55 negroes.

At the August session of the General Assembly, 1775, it was Voted and Resolved, that all the neat cattle and sheep on the Island, excepting a sufficiency for the inhabitants, be brought off as soon as possible, and landed upon the continent; that 250 men be sent to the Island to secure the stock until it could be taken off; and that the remainder of two companies in the counties of Kings and Kent, which have not marched to join the army, be employed in this service; that James Rhoades, Gideon Hoxie and George Sheffield be empowered, at the expense of the colony, to take the most prudent and effectual measures for removing the stock to the continent. Such of the stock brought off the Island as was

7

fit for that purpose, was ordered to be sent to the army under General Washington. 1908 sheep were taken from the Island. The schooner Polly was taken by the enemy while she was employed in removing stock from the Island.

At the January session of the General Assembly, 1776, an account was presented by William Greene and others for beef, hides and tallow derived from cattle taken off of this Island.

While the soldiers were at the Island, they were billeted among the inhabitants. All intercourse with the Island was forbidden. So strictly was this enforced, that when Governor William Greene was in office he had to procure the assent of the General Assembly to send a few barrels of cider to his brother-in-law, John Littlefield, who was the father of Mrs. General Greene. The records of the town were sent to Paul Niles, in Charlestown, for safe keeping, at the breaking out of the war, and for eight years after there is no entry extant to tell what they did or suffered. For eight years they were left to be preyed upon or petted alike by friend and foe, with no food to eat but such as they raised upon the Island or caught from the sea, with no clothes to wear but such as they had at the breaking out of the war, or as they could manufacture with their own hands, without a physician to heal their bodies, or a clergyman to cure their souls. The colony at intervals sent its committee to see what of fish or grain it could contribute to supply the army, and the absent landlords were permitted to return to gather their rents, and creditors were allowed in a few instances to go to look after their debtors.

At the breaking out of the war, several of the inhabitants left the Island. Ray Sands went to Tower Hill. He served as an officer during the greater part of the war. He was made a captain of the militia at the October session of the Assembly in 1775, promoted to be major in July 1776, and was made a colonel in September, 1776. His appointment to this office gave offence to Col. Segar, and at the next March session it was ascertained that his appointment had been made by mistake ; in the meantime he had defended the country from an assault from the enemy's ships. The thanks of the General Assembly were voted to him for his spirited and vigilant conduct on that occasion, and from his known zeal for the public good, the Assembly hoped and expected that he would accept the office of Lieutenant Colonel, which office he accepted.

Edward Sands removed off the Island and was chosen surgeon of an artillery regiment early in 1777.

William Littlefield, who afterwards settled in Newport, was at the October session of the Assembly, 1776, upon the recommendation of General Washington, made a first lieutenant in the new establishment of the military forces. He was the brother-in-law of General Nathanael Greene, and served afterwards as a captain in the army.

CHAPTER VI

EARLY SETTLERS.

John Alcock was born in England in 1627, graduated at Harvard College in 1646, was one of the proprietors of, and went to Block Island at its settlement, but died near Boston, March 27, 1667, five years after he went to Block Island. His estate at the Island was distributed among his children in 1677.

Simon Ray remained at the Island; his son Gideon was taken by the French and carried up the sound to the neighborhood of New York, where he remained. The descendants of Simon intermarried with the Greene family of Warwick. His grandson, Simon, married Judith Greene. Catharine Ray married William Greene, who was afterwards Governor. Some of her letters to, and from Dr. Franklin, have been published among the works of the latter. One of her sisters married Governor Samuel Ward, one married a Hubbard, of Boston, and their niece, Catharine Littlefield, daughter of John Littlefield, married General Nathanael Greene.

Philip Wharton had one child, a daughter. He left Boston, and probably joined this colony in consequence of a domestic difficulty. He separated from his family; beyond this I have not traced him.

Hugh Williams was a hatter; he joined the Boston Church January 1st, 1642. He returned to Boston; his will was dated Oct. 21st, 1674. He too, probably, had some domestic difficulties, for he gave his property to his brother John and his sister, Mrs. Hale, and an action was brought against him, while he was in life, for the defamation of his wife.

Samuel Dearing, like Simon Ray, was of Braintree. He married Mary Ray, who died in 1657, when he married Francis Newcomb. His son, Samuel, returned to Massachusetts. I think that the father remained at the Island, but the name soon became extinct.

Thomas Terry came from England in 1635 in the James. He was one of the first purchasers and settlers of the Island, and afterward removed to Freetown, in Massachusetts, where his descendants yet survive.

Thomas Faxon was of Braintree. He again returned to Braintree, was there pressed into the service under Sir William Phips in the expedition against Quebec.

Richard Ellis was from Dedham. I have no means of ascertaining what became of him; he had a daughter who married Amos Fisher of Dedham, March 12th, 1680, but I doubt if Ellis ever returned to Dedham.

Peter George was of Braintree. He had several children. He did not live long after his removal to the Island. Some of his children settled, I believe, in Newport. Commodore Stephen Decatur was one of his descendants.

William Rose, captain of the barque, soon disappeared from their records, but Thomas Rose, otherwise called Tormot Rose, who was probably son of William, remained on the Island, and has numerous descendants, many of whom followed the calling of their ancestor.

Samuel Staples was of Braintree. How long he remained at the Island I have not ascertained, but probably died there.

The mode of life of the early settlers of the Island is narrated by Mrs. Governor Greene, (Catharine Ray, Dr. Frank lin's correspondent,) in a manuscript yet extant. She derived her information from an aged relative. She says the first settlers had one cow to three families. They made mush of Indian meal, which they eat with a little milk instead of molasses. They had a fish called horse mackerel. This was their daily fare. They eat their breakfast, and went sometimes several miles to their work of clearing, and on their return this was their supper.

Speaking of her ancestor, Simon Ray, Sr., and of the mode of his torture by the French to compel him to disclose his hidden silver, she says that he was put into a cheese press and squeezed there; that at another time he was tied to a tree and whipped. Mrs. Governor Greene remembered her grandfather who died March 17th, 1737, aged 101 years, one month and one day.

Ten years before he died he made his will, distributing his estate among his children, and manumitted Esther, Sofa and Warwick, his slaves.

Mrs. Greene, and the Rev. Samuel Niles, each claims their grandfather to have been the most important man in the colony. If the records of the Island indicate who the most important member of that society was, I should say, unhesitatingly, that it was the ancestor of Mrs. Greene.

Simon Ray was a Puritan; he lived and died in the faith of the Puritans. He held public worship for very many years on Sunday at his own house. Mrs. Greene says that he had committed the New Testament and the Psalms to memory, and when he was old and blind, she heard him complaining of being ill, and that he had been able to repeat to himself but fifty chapters of the Scriptures that day.

He lies buried beneath a massive slate slab on a hill, from which a large part of the Island and the surrounding sea is in open view. The stone contains this inscription, viz:

"This monument is erected to the memory of Simon Ray, Esquire, one of the original proprietors of this Island. He was largely concerned in settling the township, and was one of its chief magistrates. Such was his benevolence that besides the care which he took of their interests, he frequently instructed them in the more important concerns of our Holy Religion. He was deprived of his eyesight many years, cheerfully submitting to the will of God, his life being in this trying instance, and all others, a lovely example of Christian virtue.
He died on the 17th of March, A. D., 1737, in the 102d year of his age."

James Danielson, sometime subsequent to 1700, went to what is now Windham county, and settled in the neighborhood of a village there which perpetuates his family name.

James Sands was born at Reading, in the county of Berkes, in England. He was one of the early settlers of Portsmouth, where he was a freeman in 1655. Mr. Sands left Portsmouth with the celebrated Ann Hutchinson, and with another person undertook the erection of a dwelling house for Mrs. Hutchinson, in the wilderness at East Chester, near New York. While he was prosecuting this undertaking, he had a singular experience with the Indians, who manifested the disposition towards him, which was afterwards developed into hostility to any settlement of their country by the whites, and which finally doomed Mrs. Hutchinson and all of her family, except a girl, a relative of her family, who was taken by the Indians, but was afterwards redeemed and married a Mr. Cole of Kingstown. Mr. Sands was driven out of the Indian country, and returned to Rhode Island—went to Taunton for a short time, and in 1663, with his wife Sarah, became one of the settlers of Block Island. He had five sons—John. James, Samuel, Edward and Job, and three daughters. The eldest of these I do not know ; the other two were Sarah and Mercy. John, James, Samuel and Job went to Long Island, and probably all settled there, at a place called Cowneck. Job married Sybil Ray, a daughter of Simon Ray, and Edward lived at Block Island, where he married Mary Williams, daughter of John, February 12th, 1685. The eldest daughter was drowned in a mill-pond, near her father's house.

Mercy Sands, the youngest daughter of Mr. James Sands, married Joshua Raymond, of New London.

James Sands died at Block Island. March 13th, 1695.

Sarah Sands, widow of James, made her will March 9th, 1699, which was proved July 6th, 1702, in which "in obedience to a promise I have made, that no child born under my protection and care shall be made a slave of, and in ratification and confirmation of this," she proceeds to provide for the bringing up and emancipation of several negro children, which is the substance of the will ; and this will, we think, fairly entitles her to be ranked among the earliest "abolitionists."

Col. Ray Sands and Captain Edward Sands were both officers in the Revolutionary army, as was their kinsman, Captain William Littlefield.

James Sands built a commodious stone house, which served the double purpose of dwelling house and fortress. The exact locality of this house is unknown to the wri-

ter. Says the Rev. Samuel Niles, in his French and Indian
Wars, "it was near a mill pond." It was not far from the
harbor, for the French, when they took possession of the
Island in 1689, "they disarmed the men and carried the
people and confined them in the house of Captain James
Sands, which was large and accommodable for their purpose,
and not far from the harbor."

When the French took the Island the third time, Sands
and his family went to the woods for shelter; their grandson,
Samuel Niles, accompanied them. They encamped in the
woods that night; the next morning Niles and Thomas
Mitchell went together to the top of a hill, where were small
bushes, and a large swamp was behind them, but they were
in fair sight of the house. From this place the French were
seen as they came up from the water side in two files. In
this manner they went to the house, and set up their standard
on a hill on the back side of it. The French fired many
guns at the house, and some of the balls whistled over Niles's
head. The landing at that time was at what is known as
"the old pier" now. The mill-pond was above what is now
known as "the upper dam," where the highway then crossed
the stream. Two of James Sands's granddaughters, sisters,
married cousins, each bearing the name of Nathaniel Littlefield. The land to the east of the mill-pond is known to
have been "Littlefield land," probably inherited from the
Sands's. If the house stood by the side of the road on the
high land east of the mill-pond, and the Niles's was located
on the hill north of "the continental swamp," the landing
place would be visible between the high-lands once occupied
by Dr. Willing's house, and the high-lands occupied by the
house of the late Joshua Littlefield ; so it is highly probable

8

that this house was located on what is now known as "the Caleb Littlefield land."

Sarah Sands, wife of James, was for a long time the doctress on the Island, and was skilled in surgery as well as in medicine. She survived her husband for several years.

James Sands, by his will, gave to his youngest son, Edward, his homestead, viz: Cow-pasture, meadow, ram-pasture, field-before-the-door, calf-pasture, great swamp and half the orchard, as they are now fenced, with the wall and all of the benefits to them belonging.

Edward Sands, by his will, dated June 13th, 1708, gave his estate to his wife for life, then to go to his daughter Sarah, but if she married Samuel Dennison she was disinherited, and the estate was to go to Edward, son of John Sands, in fee simple.

John Sands lived at Hempstead, L. I., in 1713. Samuel Sands had daughter Sybil, who married John Rogers of New London; Mercy, who married Richard Stillwell of New York; Sarah, who married Nathan Selleck of Stamford, Conn., and Ann and Mary, who were unmarried, and a son Samuel; among whom, by his will, he distributed a large estate.

John Sands married Catharine Gutterage, June 17th, 1713. They had John, January, 1798; Robert, 1710; Edward, January, 1712.

Sands's Point, on Long Island, derived its name from the Block Island Sands's, who settled there, and the New York Sands's belong to this family.

Consider Tiffany married Abagail Niles, May 27th, 1696. They had a son born June 14th, 1701. Ephraim Tiffany and wife, Bathaid, had Samuel Tiffany, born April 7th, 1707, Consider, born April 29th, 1703, and another child, born February 7th, 1707.

Samuel Arnold married Susannah George, 1706, and died insane August 9th, 1717.

Caleb Littlefield and wife, Mercy, had John Littlefield, in 1717, and John Littlefield was an ancestor of Mrs. Gen. Nathanael Greene.

Nathaniel Niles, son of John of Braintree, married Sarah, daughter of James Sands, February 14th, 1671. They had Samuel Niles, May 1, 1674 ; Nathaniel, March 21, 1677 ; Catharine, March 13th, 1680 ; Ebenezer, January 25, 1685, and Savage says a son Jeremiah.

Benjamin and John Niles were of the list of freemen in 1678, and were brothers of Nathaniel.

Samuel Niles, son of Nathaniel, was the first graduate of Harvard College from Rhode Island. The elder Adams said he was in the list of the excellent and worthy men whom he knew among the ministers of New England who were all men of learning—pious, humble, prudent, faithful and useful men in their day, and "that in his youth he revered, and still reveres, this honest, virtuous and pious man."

Samuel Niles was first settled in 1699 at Block Island. He preached in South Kingstown from 1702 to 1710. He was settled at Braintree, August 23d, 1711. His first wife was a daughter of Peter Thatcher of Milton, whom he married in 1716. His second wife was Ann Coddington, whom he married in 1732. In 1745 he published a brief and sorrowful account of the churches in New England. In 1752 he published a vindication of diverse important doctrines of Scripture. In 1757, "Scripture doctrines of Original Sin." He also wrote a History of the Indian and French wars, which was published in the 3d series Mass. Hist. Coll. Vol. VI. His son was the Hon. Samuel Niles of Braintree, and the Rev. Samuel Niles, of Abington, was his grandson. The Hon. Nathaniel Niles of Vermont, who is said to have been born in South Kingstown, in 1741, was of this family. He was a judge, a member of Congress, and the author of "The American Hero," a sapphic ode, which was set to music, and was the war song of the Revolution.

The first Samuel Niles was first settled as minister at the Island in 1699, but did not remain there in that capacity but one or two years.

William G. Angell was born in a house, late the residence of Josiah Sheffield, and which was removed by him several years since, a short distance to the west of its former site, where it is now the residence of Mr. Edmund B. Peckham. Mr. Angell removed to Burlington, in Otsego county, in the State of New York, from which place he was elected a representative in Congress in 1825, and was re-elected in 1829.

Gideon Olin resided in the same house, which was afterwards occupied by William G. Angell. Mr. Olin removed to and became one of the founders of Vermont, where he was a member of the legislature, Speaker of the House of Representatives, a Judge of the County Court, and from which he was elected to Congress in 1803, and re-elected in 1805.

Jeremiah Briggs and Nathaniel Briggs, long distinguished shipping merchants, under the firm of J. & N. Briggs, in the city of New York, were both natives of Block Island.

The topography of this Island is peculiar ; it resembles

the sea running high before a northeast gale, and suggests that the Island may have been thrown up in some convulsion of nature, and have taken its form from the waves which it penetrated. During the revolutionary war it was stripped of its trees. Its soil is fertile, and the enterprise of its inhabitants has carried culture to every hill-top, and there is little of its surface that is left to waste. The chain of ponds that extend across the Island is picturesque. But the most attractive place to me are the high banks on the south side of the Island. Those rude gray cliffs, which, since their creation, or possibly since the morning stars first sang together for joy, have presented their bared breasts in battle array to the sea and storm, always had a mysterious attraction to me. In my youth no neighboring dwelling or other intrusion came to interrupt the converse of the surrounding scenes with the soul of the solitary visitor. There I saw in the swelling and recession of the mighty bosom of the sea, the respiration of God in nature ; there in the calm and lull of the elements, I heard "the still small voice" fall upon my ears, wooing from above all that was good within me, and in the thunder and earthquake shock of the storm, I have often stood, almost paralyzed, under the spell-binding influence of the warning voice thus coming from that Power which had aroused the wrath of the forces of nature, and was breaking forth in the war of the elements. There I have seen the strong ship which had traversed every zone, crushed by the power of the ocean wave as if her sides were but wisps of straw, and been impressed with the utter powerlessness of man to contend with him who holds the sea in the hollow of His hand, and with His will directs the storm. Then there, when the reason wearied in grappling with these higher thoughts, gave way, the mingling of memory and the

musings of the imagination peopled the mind with creations
of the fancy moulded in forms of loveliness and beauty, the
genial companions of an ardent and hopeful youth, took possession of the soul, but then departed forever at the sum-
mons to encounter the hard realities of active life, and left
no trace of their existence but the remembrance of the en-
thusiasm they had aroused.

I have gleaned the facts which I have here narrated
from the obscure records of this ancient township,
from the colonial records, from books that are accessible, and
from those that are almost inaccessible, from ancestral grave-
stones and private papers, from traditions, some of which I
listened to, and read even before I could comprehend their
import, from a knowledge of every field, and an acquaintance
with every family which has inhabited this Island for the last
fifty years.   And I have been stimulated to these investiga-
tions by the fact that the blood of the founders of this Island
has descended to my children, and that I first saw the light
on the territory consecrated by the privations and toil of the
settlers of this lovely Island.

www.ingramcontent.com/pod-product-compliance
Lightning Source LLC
Chambersburg PA
CBHW021535270326
41930CB00008B/1255